The Beaver Book of Ballet

If you're a ballet student and keen to improve
your dancing, you'll know how important it is
to practise regularly and to understand exactly
what you're doing and why. This book explains
how the exercises you do in class (illustrated for
home practice) prepare you for dancing different steps, and looks at the way in which the
style of dancing we call ballet has changed and
developed over the years. It examines the
training of a would-be dancer and careers in the
ballet world, and finally, gives lists of music
and books for the keen student and a Glossary
of ballet terms.

Robina Beckles Willson is the author of
several books for children. She has also written
many stories, three of which are included in
The Beaver Book of Bedtime Stories.

The Beaver Book of Ballet

Robina Beckles Willson

Illustrated by Shirley Soar

Beaver Books

First published in 1979 by
The Hamlyn Publishing Group Limited
London · New York · Sydney · Toronto
Astronaut House, Feltham, Middlesex, England

© Copyright Text Robina Beckles Willson 1979
© Copyright Illustrations
The Hamlyn Publishing Group Limited 1979
ISBN 0 600 31517 7

Set, printed and bound in Great Britain by
Cox & Wyman Limited, Reading
Set in Monotype Garamond

Contents

Acknowledgement

Many people have helped and advised me as
I prepared this book, but I should particularly
like to thank the following at the junior
department of the Royal Ballet School:
Ms Pauline Wadsworth, Mr Richard Glasstone,
and all the pupils whose classes I attended
and who answered my questions. I am also
grateful to Ms Rosemary Andrews, Ms Eileen
Meacock, Sarah Rowland and Richard Wilde.

Finally, I have much appreciated the work
of Catherine Burchill, who typed the manu-
script, and Joanna Nettleton (ex Royal
Ballet), who read and checked it for me.

R.B.W.

The publishers are grateful to Mr James
Monahan, Director, and Ms Barbara Fewster,
Director of Balletic Studies, both of the
Royal Ballet School, for permission to
photograph classes.

1 What is ballet?

Ballet is much more than dancing. It is an art, combining dancing with music and drama as entertainment for an audience. This performance is supported by costumes and scenery.

The history of ballet

In a short outline of ballet's history, it is possible to pick out people who have been leaders, making bold changes or steadily improving old accepted forms. These important pioneers were not always dancers, although, of course, dancers were the interpreters of new

A class of eager young dancers hard at work

ideas and experiments. Because ballet is a blend of other arts, new impulses have sometimes come from musicians or composers, from artists, actors and poets, from teachers or those able to find and mould talent to its best advantage in ballet. When considerable talents have worked well together, masterpieces have been created.

The history of ballet can be seen as one of traditions handed down from teacher to pupil. Even today, when films can record dancing exactly, and a way of writing down movements has been successfully established (see page 75), ballet dancing stays alive by the passing down of what has been learned, from demonstrating and copying on the studio floor. You learn from what you are shown by your teacher and the corrections she suggests. She teaches what was passed on to her.

Dancing is a primitive instinct, moving to express feeling and to make magic. To dance for pleasure is an old custom, although we cannot now know exactly how, for instance, the ancient Greeks and Romans danced. We can only guess from their paintings, sculptures and documents.

Although it inherits qualities from earlier times, ballet's history can be traced from the sixteenth century. It began as a court spectacle. The first ballet of which we have record was *Le Ballet Comique de la Reine* (The Queen's Comedy Ballet), given in 1581 to celebrate the wedding of the sister of Queen Catherine de Medici of France.

Some ideas were adapted from spectacles in Italy and masques in England, and the ballet lasted nearly six hours. The audience numbered over nine thousand people. The novelty of this performance was that it told a story, with various dances and interludes, using elaborate scenery.

Up to that time, court entertainment had consisted of courtiers dancing to form intricate patterns, with their movements watched from above, from the throne and a raised platform. In this wedding celebration in 1581, ladies danced for the first time, forming a sort of chorus. Dancing, singing, recitation and spectacle were all mixed together.

The dancers at court were amateurs, but they were expert, having plenty of time to give to this elegant pastime. Sometimes the public were admitted to their performances, and in 1636 the first public theatre was opened in France.

Louis XIV dressed as the Sun for a court ballet

In 1643, Louis XIV came to the throne. Like earlier French kings, he was an enthusiastic dancer, and enjoyed taking part in court ballets. He had various dancing masters. It was one of these, Beauchamp, who probably persuaded him to bring outside professional dancers into his court entertainments.

These outside dancers were acrobats and tumblers, wandering players and gipsies, who performed in fairgrounds and villages. In fairground dances, women had taken part. And neither men nor women had been constricted by court dignity or formal, heavy clothes.

When they were allowed into court entertainment, these professional dancers brought vigour and new life. At that time the composer Lully (1633–87) was writing music for ballets which introduced comedies by the playwright, Molière. Molière's plays often had dancing interludes between the scenes too, and were very popular. Good miming and acting was important, and the dancers were expected to act too. Molière worked to bring comedy, music and ballet together.

Ballet gradually became a professional entertainment, and in 1661 Louis XIV founded a school for training dancers, which is still in existence today, at the Opéra in Paris. It was called L'Académie Royale de Danse (The Royal Academy of Dancing). The first members were thirteen dancing masters to the King, his Queen, and various members of the aristocracy. Lully was one of the directors of the Academy. He was a composer, a dancer and a conductor too. His work demonstrates the close relationship between dancing and music, as ballet developed.

Beauchamp, who was ballet master to the new Academy, named the five positions of the feet (see page 34) and began to work out the technique which became the foundation of ballet as we know it today. Italian masters had taught their dancing pupils to turn their feet outwards slightly. Beauchamp continued this trend, and practice to gain freer movement made it a characteristic of ballet (see page 33, Turn-out).

Louis XIV drew up the rules for his Dancing Academy himself. Because this French Academy was the first one to study and develop ballet, the names of steps and movements were given in French. This custom survives today, and when you learn ballet technique, the terms will be in French. This language is used by all ballet dancers, and enables them to understand the instructions of teachers all over the world. (See page 88 onwards for the Glossary. Not all the French terms have an exact English equivalent, but you will find their meanings in the Glossary.)

Some famous names in the early days of ballet

The early days of ballet are peopled with many fascinating characters.

La Camargo (1710–70) was trained from the age of ten in Paris. She became famous as a dancer because she shortened her skirt (which was considered daring) and removed the heels from her dancing slippers. The new freedom of a shortened skirt and simpler footwear gave her the opportunity to develop a more brilliant dancing technique.

Up to that time, stage machinery had sometimes been used to carry dancers and make them look as if they were flying, but now more elaborate jumps and footwork could be used. La Camargo also introduced an early form of the *entrechat*. This is the movement of the feet crossing and re-crossing during a jump, and La Camargo perfected the *entrechat quatre*, in which the feet change place twice in the air so that the dancer lands with the same foot in front as when she started. (For the development of the *entrechat*, see page 21.)

La Camargo

La Sallé

La Camargo was admired for her lightness and quick movements and, as you can see from the picture, she turned her feet out at ninety degrees. (See page 33, Turn-out.) She danced so well that she was considered to be the equal of a man – high praise at that time!

La Camargo's great rival was **La Sallé** (1707–56), whose dancing style was more graceful and less aerial. La Sallé in her turn tried to free the dancer from heavy clothes, and set an example by wearing Greek draperies in a ballet called *Pygmalion*. However, this was considered so shocking that the experiment was not repeated until the time of the American, Isadora Duncan (1878–1927.)

La Sallé was an acrobat's daughter, and first danced in public at a fairground, at the age of eleven. Her first appearance at the Opéra in Paris was at fourteen, and she retired when she was thirty-three.

As the dancers' legs and feet were now in view, for some time the emphasis was on the technical marvels which dancers could accomplish. This new skill was greatly admired. Ballets were not dramatic entertainments, but consisted of a series of striking entrances and diversions by the dancers. A famous teacher then came forward to adjust the balance of the ballet in his teaching and writing.

Jean-Georges Noverre (1727–1810) claimed that ballet must not be used just as an excuse for dancing brilliantly, but it should also express a dramatic idea. He stressed the importance of a dancer being able to 'speak' with his or her hands and face and eyes, so that the work was living, not mechanical. His ideas were much admired by the English actor-manager, David Garrick, who called him 'The Shakespeare of the dance'. Garrick encouraged Noverre to use more mime in ballet to express feelings, where there had been merely the copying of complicated steps and movements from ballet to ballet.

Noverre also attacked the frequent use of masks by dancers. In **La Guimard** (1743–1816), he found an ideal dancer who was an excellent mime, and concentrated on that rather than a showy technique. At the age of sixty-four, however, La Guimard gave a farewell performance to her friends with a lowered curtain, so that only her legs and feet could be seen. Perhaps she felt that they looked younger than her face.

Auguste Vestris

Auguste Vestris (1760–1842) was the leading dancer at the Paris Opéra for thirty-six years, and he developed technical skill, particularly in elevation (jumping), to such an extent that his father said: 'It is only out of pity for his dancing friends that my son agrees to touch the ground.'

Carlo Blasis (1797–1878) was an Italian who followed Noverre in developing the ballet in his writing and teaching. He started his career as a dancer at twelve, and was a choreographer and dancer at the King's Theatre, London, for a time.

He studied sculpture and anatomy and was able to explain clearly the workings of ballet technique. In his *Treatise on the Art of Dancing* (1820), he made plain the science of dancing. Blasis devised the *attitude* (see page 45), a pose based on a statue of the winged god, Mercury. When in 1837 he became director of the Academy of Dancing at Milan, he made rules which are still copied in many ballet schools today. His pupils were admitted after eight and before twelve years old, or fourteen if they were boys. They had three hours' dancing practice and one hour of mime each day. The school was so famous that its influence spread to France and to Russia.

Blasis had a pupil, Giovanni Lepri. Lepri's pupil, **Enrico Cecchetti** (1850–1928), taught many famous dancers, teachers and directors, such as Pavlova, Massine, Ninette de Valois and Marie Rambert. These were the connections that link yesterday's ballet with today's, even though styles and aims have varied so much from generation to generation. Blasis developed a technique by which a dancer could measure herself or himself. His system of aiming for a pure line and fluent movement is the basis of classical dancing. The next phase of ballet brought changes in aims and ideas.

We have pictures and descriptions of these early dancers and their work, but today there is a new practical interest in early dance. Just as musicians have studied surviving early instruments, and copied them to play today, so dance historians have tried to re-create early dances, from as early as the twelfth century onwards. You may be lucky enough to see performances of early court and ballet dancing as it was first seen. Look out for them. You may even find that you can attend a course of demonstrations and learn some of the movements and steps yourself (see page 86).

Marie Taglioni

Fanny Elssler

Carlotta Grisi

Romantic ballet

The first version of the ballet *La Sylphide* was produced in 1832, and with this the Romantic movement in ballet began. The same characteristics were found in the music of Liszt, Chopin, Schumann and Wagner, and the writings of Scott, Byron and Hugo.

Instead of myths and country scenes dramatic stories, with the atmosphere of fairy tales and ballads, were told. Long white net dresses caught rays of moonlight on darkened stages. Atmosphere was crucial. Billowing dresses hid the effort of the dancers' legs and made the sylphs seem to glide rather than dance in an enchanted grove. The dancers began to rise on their toes in flat slippers, to give the impression of lightness and flight. La Camargo had jumped, but **Marie Taglioni** (1804–84), as La Sylphide, seemed to float – a creature of the air, a sylph or spirit.

Marie Taglioni inspired such adoration that the poet, Gautier, who led the new Romantic movement in ballet, declared that he was fearful for her life, she was showered with so many flowers at the first night of *La Sylphide*. Taglioni was born in Stockholm, taught by her father, and trained in Paris from the age of eight. However, she did not stay in Paris, but travelled all over Europe and was immensely popular in Russia. Queen Victoria enjoyed ballet, and had dolls dressed in costumes which Taglioni wore in various roles.

Technically, Taglioni took ballet another step forward by strapping her toes for extra support and darning the ends of her shoes. Then she was able to dance on the tips of her toes, and enhance the lightness for which she was admired.

Romantic ballet glorified the ballerina. Male dancers became useful only to lift and support, again to flatter the grace and lightness of their partners. Only in Russia, and in national dancing, did the men keep an equal status with women.

Taglioni had a great rival, **Fanny Elssler** (1810–84). Critics took sides as to who was the better dancer, making ballet and the adoration of ballerinas ever more popular. In fact, the two dancers had contrasting talents. Elssler borrowed steps from Spain and dances from Hungary and Poland. Her feet seemed to cut into the stage, whereas Taglioni's hardly touched the boards.

A third great ballerina of this period was **Carlotta Grisi** (1818–99), for whom *Giselle*, the ballet still loved and performed today, was made. She came to France from Italy, and combined the dramatic and technical qualities needed to act and dance the demanding part.

Ballet in Russia

Russian dancers visited Louis XIV's court in France. Peter the Great (1672–1725) introduced social dancing in Russia, and the Empress Anne (1693–1740) founded an academy which still exists, choosing a French director. Other French and Italian teachers followed, and dancers such as Taglioni were welcomed.

Russian ballet could choose its companies from the many folk dancers who had traditionally entertained wealthy Russian nobles. Male dancers were especially strong and vigorous, and brought these qualities into the Russian version of ballet, based on the French tradition. From 1857 to 1910 **Marius Petipa**, born in France, ruled over the ballet at the Maryinsky Theatre in Saint Petersburg, now Leningrad. He helped to create over sixty full-length ballets. Only three survive, to Tchaikovsky's music: *Swan Lake*, *The Sleeping Beauty* and *Nutcracker*. These are considered great classical ballets, and you may often see them performed today.

Enrico Cecchetti (see page 15) also came to Russia from Italy to give his brilliant teaching talents to the Russian ballet.

Another visitor to Russia was an American, **Isadora Duncan**

Isadora Duncan

(1878–1927), who arrived in 1905. Although she admired some ballerinas, Isadora felt that classical ballet had become rigid and artificial, merely showing off technique. She chose to dance to music which had, up to that time, only been considered suitable for performance in concert halls (for example works by Bach and Wagner). Using this music to help her convey dramatic ideas, she moved her body freely, not with accepted classical steps and mime. Her feet were bare and, as La Sallé (see page 13), Isadora wore flowing draperies as she tried to express the meaning of the music in her own inspired style of dance. All this made a tremendous impression of something fresh and daring.

There were other people at this time who felt that ballet needed a change of direction, even if they did not go to such extremes as Isadora. One was a young choreographer. **Michael Fokine** (1880–1942) had created ballets such as *The Dying Swan* (1907) and *Chopiniana* (later called *Les Sylphides*, 1908). These were admired by the artist, **Alexandre Benois**, who, with friends, produced a paper called *The World of Art*. They were trying to show Russia to the West, and also to learn from the West themselves.

When they saw the Italian ballerina, **Virginia Zucchi** (1847–1930), they began to imagine new possibilities in ballet as an art. Benois,

Virginia Zucchi

who was to design costumes and scenery, said that her dancing gave him an ecstasy of delight. Her picture somehow looks modern, and she certainly helped to launch the new movement which became modern ballet.

The virtuosity of such dancers as Zucchi caused the ballet dress to be shortened to the brief version shown here. You can see at once that it is a demanding costume for a dancer. The bodice needs a controlled body. It must fit snugly at the waist, but leave room over the ribs for bending and breathing. Your arms have to balance the sticking-out skirt. You cannot see your own feet, but an audience can see every movement of your legs.

This classical tutu was popular in the 1880s in Russia. The name 'tutu' was also given to the longer, bell-shaped skirt as worn in *La Sylphide*, which was cut off below the knees – a much less spectacular style.

The tutu is made with layers of net or tarlatan. The garment consists of a fitted bodice, which may be boned, a basque below the waist, and panties, trimmed with four or five rows of frills, one over the other, each deeper than the last, and two wider frills on top. There are variations, and one layer can be wired. When you wear a short tutu you are following a tradition from Zucchi's time.

The tutu

It was considered seemly to cover bare legs with tights when skirts were so short or transparent. Maillot (died c. 1838) a costumier at the Paris Opéra at the beginning of the nineteenth century, is said to have invented tights, and the French have given his name (*maillot*) to this garment. But it is likely that similar stockings with pants were used before his time, and the painting of Zucchi with her upturned skirt, shown on the previous page, looks as if she is wearing tights.

Fokine wished to reform ballet, and experimented by reducing the use of pointe work and even writing a ballet for dancing in bare feet. He wanted ballet movements to fit the subject and the music and not to be set steps. He felt that the whole of the dancer's body should be expressive, not just the hands and face. Fokine was a painter and musician himself, and he wanted the musician and the scene painter to work on equal terms with the dancers.

Such ideals needed great talent. Two brilliant dancers were emerging: Anna Pavlova (1881–1931) and Vaslav Nijinsky (1890–1950).

These people were brought together, and the dancers, teachers, artists and musicians led by **Sergei Diaghilev** (1872–1929). He had organised exhibitions of Russian works in Paris, and had taken Russian music and opera there too. When Benois interested him in ballet he at first hoped to be able to present it at the Imperial Theatres. But quarrels and enemies drove him from working in Russia, and in 1909 he took a Russian ballet company to Paris.

The Russians enjoyed overwhelming success there and in England and America. **Vaslav Nijinsky** was the first male Russian dancer to be seen in Europe at that period. He was an individual dancer, adored as only ballerinas had been before. A famous role was *Le Spectre de la Rose* (The Spirit of the Rose), when he made a breathtaking leap from the window after dancing with a young girl, as the spirit of a red rose she wore to her first ball. His elevation looked effortless, and he could do an *entrechat huit* (eight) or even *entrechat dix* (ten) (see page 12).

Nijinsky, also under Diaghilev's guidance, attempted choreography, and one of his ballets was *L'Après-midi d'un Faune* (The Afternoon of a Faun). This was an attempt to show a primitive creature and imitate the figures in Greek paintings, turning the body and head in profile, and using jerky movements.

Vaslav Nijinsky

This ballet caused a scandal and was widely disapproved of at first. Another experimental ballet choreographed by Nijinsky, *Le Sacré du Printemps* (The Rite of Spring), in which he took part, also caused an uproar at its first performance in 1913. Sadly, Nijinsky's experiments away from classical ballet technique and his entire dancing career came to an end when he had a mental breakdown, starting in 1916. His last solo performance was in 1919.

The Diaghilev Ballet At first, dancers joined Diaghilev during their vacations from Russia to tour in Europe. But gradually Diaghilev drew round himself a company which he directed for twenty years. They eventually made a base in Monte Carlo, and Polish dancers joined the Russian dancers he engaged. Lydia Sokolova was the first English dancer who, in 1912, became one of his ballerinas. Other English members of his company were Alicia Markova, Anton Dolin, Ninette de Valois (see also page 28) and Marie Rambert (see also page 26).

Diaghilev had a magnetic personality. He brought back Cecchetti to train his dancers. He attracted artists such as Bakst and Picasso to paint his sets. Stravinsky wrote ballet scores for him throughout the life of the Diaghilev Ballet. With all these chosen talents Diaghilev collaborated to form a complete work of art for the theatre. He was difficult to work with, but had such skill in inspiring ideas and drawing out schemes that he was able to advise musicians as they composed, painters as they painted, choreographers as they invented ballets, and designers as they made costumes, and bring all their talents together. He gave personal attention to many details, and supervised stage lighting with endless patience.

Diaghilev's company was called 'Les Ballets Russes' (The Russian Ballets) – it is useful to keep this French name, to distinguish it from the traditional Russian Ballet, which continued in Russia, and still does today.

After Nijinsky left his company, Diaghilev found a new young dancer in the Moscow School, Leonide Massine (b. 1895). He started as a soloist in 1914, but in only one year started to create ballets as a choreographer too. Massine made many experiments. He learnt the technique of Spanish gipsy dancing to use it in *The Three-Cornered Hat*. In *La Boutique Fantasque* (The Magic Toyshop) he used material from Italy, Russia and France. The toys who came to life were given characters in their dancing in a way which was new to ballet, and he brought comedy into dancing. Massine danced and taught all over the world, including the Royal Ballet School as a guest teacher of choreography in 1969.

Bronislava Nijinska (1891–1972), Nijinsky's sister, became a choreographer as well as a teacher when Massine left Diaghilev's company. A work still performed today is *Les Noces* (The Wedding Ritual), to music by Stravinsky. She helped to train Serge Lifar (b. 1905), another choreographer who worked with Diaghilev and later the Paris Opéra. Nijinska also taught Frederick Ashton (b. 1904), a leading choreographer working in England today. Balanchine (b. 1904) created ballets for Diaghilev, and later founded the American Ballet in New York.

In 1921, Diaghilev brought back a full length production of *The Sleeping Beauty*, to Tchaikovsky's music, adapting a production from his youth in Imperial Russia. Although it was not a commercial success in London, audiences who had seen it and the one-act version of *Swan Lake* did not again forget the great classical ballets, which had been ignored in the dazzling new experiments Diaghilev had presented to his public.

Diaghilev's influence on the history of ballet is almost impossible to exaggerate. This influence lives on in the teachers and dancers who worked with him, and have been able to pass on something of the spirit of 'Les Ballets Russes'.

Anna Pavlova Anna Pavlova (1881–1931) was a delicate child, born in St Petersburg (now called Leningrad). Before she was eight, she was determined to become a dancer. This ambition was awakened by seeing *The Sleeping Beauty*. When she was ten she competed with nearly a hundred children for seven or eight places, and was accepted into the Russian Imperial School. Pavlova was an unusual dancer because she looked frail, even when she became healthy and strong as a young woman. Her arms and legs were long and slim, and she moved her head gracefully. Her face was expressive rather than beautiful, and she danced many roles, including brilliant Spanish and Mexican dances, a superb Giselle, and Fokine's famous ballet *The Dying Swan* (1907), which no one since has been able to dance in the same way.

Anna Pavlova

Pavlova's personality was very attractive to audiences, and her career was a long list of successes. She appeared first at the Maryinski Theatre in 1889, but was able to travel abroad with her own company by 1908, and to Riga, Scandinavia and Germany. She visited Berlin in 1909, and London and America the following year.

Diaghilev himself was inspired by Pavlova's successes to try his first season in Paris, which she joined, in 1909. Pavlova danced across the first Ballets Russes poster, but she only stayed with that company for their first season, returning as a guest in London performances in 1911.

Pavlova left Diaghilev's company because the critics' praise for the exciting new dancer, Vaslav Nijinsky, seemed to overshadow her. Also Diaghilev was supporting a new discovery, Ida Rubenstein (1885–1960), and Pavlova did not agree with all his modern experiments.

So Pavlova became the leader of a touring company, and a major influence in her own right – in fact a legend while she was still alive. Hundreds of people who saw Pavlova longed to become dancers and to imitate her in their dancing and teaching. She herself was taught for many years by Cecchetti, and was a perfectionist, giving attention to the smallest details. When Russian and Polish dancers in her company quarrelled, she replaced them with English girls, whom she found more meek and obedient! Perhaps English ballet teachers today might not agree! When Pavlova was alive she overshadowed everyone in her company, but when she died she left a group of well trained young dancers, who did much to spread excellence in England and elsewhere.

Ballet in Britain

England had provided enthusiastic audiences for ballet in the eighteenth century, and by the end of the nineteenth century it was mainly found as an act in music-halls, mostly performed by foreign ballerinas.

There had been a long established Royal Danish Ballet, and Adeline Genée (1878–1970) was very popular in England from 1897 until she retired in 1917. She died in England and was really a Danish-British dancer. She was the first President of the Royal

Academy of Dancing (founded in 1920), succeeded in 1954 by Margot Fonteyn.

The popularity of Diaghilev's company gave English audiences an idea of the exciting possibilities in ballet. Pavlova and her company demonstrated its beauty.

In 1932, Les Ballets Russes was reformed in Monte Carlo by Colonel de Basil (1888–1951), who took the company on world tours until his death. His 'baby ballerinas', Toumanova, Baronova and Riabouchinska, started a fashion, and encouraged many English and other children to start dancing. Tamara Toumanova, who first performed in public at nine, had herself been inspired by Pavlova.

Two outstanding English dancers from Diaghilev's company did not stay with the de Basil company after Diaghilev's death. They became leading pioneers of English ballet, forming from English dancers companies which had their own individual strengths and styles.

Marie Rambert The chief contribution to ballet made by Marie Rambert (b. 1888) might be said to be her ability to draw out the talents of others. Before she joined Diaghilev's company she had studied Dalcroze eurythmics, a system of movement to music. She did not dance for long, but gathered round her some brilliant young English dancers, long before it was accepted in England that English dancers could do well. It was sometimes forgotten that Alicia Markova (b. 1910), who started with Diaghilev at fourteen and who was then dancing in England as a star ballerina, was English, born Lillian Alicia Marks.

Marie Rambert presented some public performances by her students from 1927, and then in 1931 founded the Ballet Club, in buildings which became the Mercury Theatre in London. It was a small theatre company and school combined. Here Marie Rambert found and nurtured the talent of Frederick Ashton, the choreographer who has produced a steady stream of nearly a hundred works since that time. Ashton had been to ballet classes with Massine, in Ida Rubenstein's company, and Marie Rambert had been taught by Nijinska – again links with Diaghilev's company.

Marie Rambert has discovered and encouraged other choreographers too, and has always been willing to experiment. Many dancers, such as Harold Turner, Diane Gould and Pearl Argyle, started with Rambert. Because her theatre was small, she could afford to try out productions which a larger theatre could not risk, in case it lost a great deal of money.

For some time, from about 1953, there was a Rambert Educational School for children from eight, and in 1978 the Rambert Academy for dancers from sixteen to nineteen was founded at the West London Institute. Today ballet students may be taken from the age of sixteen to join a small company, which tours energetically in Great Britain and abroad. It has kept up a tradition of experiment, and now produces striking new and modern ballets. In such works, you will see the extreme of simplicity in ballet dress – the body tights. In these the dancer's slightest movement is revealed. The body is only masked and not hidden.

Marie Rambert's young dancers were pleasing ballet audiences before de Basil brought his 'baby ballerinas' to London in 1933. Some of her dancers did join de Basil, but the competition from abroad did not stop English ballet from developing its own character.

Ballet Rambert in Glen Tetley's
Embrace Tiger and Return to Mountain

Ninette de Valois Only the barest outline can be given of the enormous contribution which Ninette de Valois (b. 1898) has made to English ballet, as a dancer, a choreographer and a teacher with a genius for organisation.

Ninette started as a child prodigy, and spent two years in Diaghilev's company, dancing and studying. Then, in 1926, she founded her own dancing school. She also worked in Cambridge and Dublin as a producer from 1929, taking her pupils to perform in plays and operas there and at the Old Vic in London. This gave her a grasp of the need for ballet to be effective theatre for its audiences.

Ninette de Valois, together with Marie Rambert, Arnold Haskell (b. 1903) and others founded the Camargo Society in 1930, to promote and support English ballet. Her productions attracted the attention of Lillian Baylis of the Old Vic Theatre, who invited de Valois to join her with her pupils, and form a ballet company. With considerable daring, de Valois accepted the invitation, and gave up her school, taking six girls and another teacher with her. The Sadlers Wells theatre in Islington was converted from an old country house into a new base, with a studio built for the dancers. Markova and Dolin were invited as guests, and gradually the Vic-Wells Ballet became known and successful, starting by giving dances in operas and later developing its own work.

Robert Helpmann, born 1909 in Australia and a director of ballet there from 1965 to 1976, was 'discovered' by de Valois when he came to London in 1933. He had also studied with Pavlova's company, when they toured Australia. He studied at the Vic-Wells Ballet and became a leading dancer, a choreographer, and an actor on stage and in films. Another leading 'star' trained by de Valois was Margot Fonteyn (b. 1919), who gave to English ballet its own, home-grown ballerina, who still delights audiences all over the world today.

At first these ballet students were taught by a tutor, but eventually, in 1947, a school providing general education as well as ballet was founded by Ninette de Valois. In 1948 boys followed the first girls. As the school grew, larger buildings were needed, and the children under sixteen moved out from London to Richmond Park.

In 1956, Queen Elizabeth II granted the Sadlers Wells Ballet and Sadlers Wells School a royal charter. So now they are known by the names Royal Ballet, and Royal Ballet School. A separate company, the Sadlers Wells Royal Ballet, is based at the Royal Opera House.

London Festival Ballet This company was founded in 1950, and named after the Festival of Britain of 1951. Its main London home is at the Festival Hall on the south bank of the river Thames, but it has toured a great deal with new and old ballets and is directed by Beryl Grey. She trained at the Sadlers Wells Ballet School, and danced solos from the early age of fifteen.

The Scottish Ballet These dancers are also directed by a dancer who was once at Sadlers Wells, Peter Darrell (b. 1929). At first, the company was called the Western Theatre Ballet, and its aim was to introduce ballet to parts of Great Britain where people seldom had the chance to see live ballet. The Scottish Ballet has performed some ballets with modern themes. It revives the classical ballets too, to give audiences as wide a range as possible.

There are other, smaller touring groups which you may be able to see, such as the Northern Dance Theatre, based in Manchester. They have been coached by Alicia Markova, a direct link with Diaghilev, for whom she danced. Dancing groups form and reform, so look out for them wherever you live. If you visit Ireland you can see the Irish Ballet, directed by Domy Reiter-Soffer.

American ballet

The links between old traditions and ballet today can be seen in America too, where there is an explosion of ballet activity, which has been called dance fever.

The Philadelphia Ballet was the first American company to visit Europe, in 1937. George Balanchine (b. 1904) used his experience with Diaghilev and de Basil as the first director of American Ballet, in 1935, based in New York. The Russian Mikhail Baryshnikov joined his New York City Ballet in 1978. The American Ballet Theatre, formed in 1939, has produced its own version of classical ballet with true American verve. An early success was *Fancy Free* (1944), by their choreographer and dancer, Jerome Robbins (b. 1918), to music by Bernstein. This was made into a musical, *On the Town*. In 1957 Robbins again collaborated with Bernstein to produce the marvellous musical and film, *West Side Story*, which contains some really exciting dancing.

The American Ballet Theatre in Fancy Free

Anthony Dowell (b. 1943), trained at the Royal Ballet School and a leading dancer in its company, is now visiting the American Ballet Theatre.

America has sent her ambassadors for ballet back to Great Britain, partly in her musicals, and also in her modern dance, influencing many small groups and companies, especially the London Contemporary Dance Theatre.

The American, Isadora Duncan (see page 18), inspired Ruth St Denis, a teacher of dance. She in turn inspired Martha Graham (b. 1894), who led her own company in experiments to free dance from what seemed to her to be restrictions in classical training.

Norman Morrice (b. 1931) studied with Martha Graham and then composed modern ballets for the Ballet Rambert. He now directs the Royal Ballet. The American, Glen Tetley (b. 1926), has also made ballets for the Rambert. These in turn have influenced the Rambert's associate director and choreographer, Christopher Bruce (b. 1945).

Old and new companies interchange, and, with the ease of modern travel, influence each other closely and quickly. To gain such artistic freedom to travel, study others and change companies, Rudolph Nureyev (b. 1938) daringly left Russia in 1961, to dance in Europe. Since that time, he has enriched world ballet with colossal energy and talent, directing as well as dancing. Others have followed, such as Natalia Makarova (b. 1940), who left Russian ballet in 1970 and now belongs to the American Ballet Theatre, although she visits England. In 1978 Mikhail Baryshnikov joined the New York City Ballet. But the movement is not only one-way. In 1978, two English dancers were invited to train with the Russian Bolshoi Company.

Today people move about in a way which would have staggered earlier dancers, making leisurely progress by train and boat. An English composer, Peter Maxwell-Davies, for instance, has collaborated with a Danish choreographer, Flemming Flindt, in Denmark. Late in 1978 they produced *Salome*, in a huge old circus building in Copenhagen. Their aim was to attract audiences in thousands – people who had never seen ballet and might enjoy dramatic dance theatre based on the Bible story of Salome and John the Baptist.

Today, there are ballet companies all over the world. Many of them tour, so that in London, for instance, we can see Danish, Russian, Japanese, Indian, Israeli and Scottish dancers, all in one year, and learn from them. Films and television also carry performances of dances wherever people wish to see them. Ballet schools are international in their pupils. Teachers take their ideas to new students in courses overseas. There is an international exchange of art and experience.

In an outline of the history of ballet only a few stars from the constellation of dancers who have dazzled audiences can be described. When you read more you will find whole books dedicated to pictures and accounts of the famous leaders of ballet.

Yet even in this short account it becomes clear that dancers have often created their own ballets, as choreographers. They have created the next generation as teachers. It is a closely knit chain. Dancers are like an extraordinary family, which is now winged and can fly from one part of the world to another.

2 What makes a ballet dancer?

Several different qualities are needed of a good dancer – he or she must have a feeling for music and acting ability as well as perfect technique. This chapter takes a look at the physical, musical and dramatic aspects of ballet and how they depend on each other.

The body: classical ballet technique

The main difference between classical ballet technique and other dancing techniques is the use of turn-out.

The dancer's legs must always be turned out as well as the feet

Turn-out should be used all the time. In this way the legs can be raised higher in any direction and a more graceful line obtained than would otherwise be the case

Turn-out Not only the foot, but the whole leg from the hip down must be turned out, including the thigh, knee and ankle. Whatever step is being danced and however the dancer's legs are placed, they must always be turned out fully.

One reason for the use of turn-out in classical ballet can be found in its early history (see also page 9). King Louis XIV of France (1638–1715) was devoted to dancing. He had a daily lesson with Pierre Beauchamp (1639–1705), his dancing master, who introduced the idea of turn-out. Early in Louis XIV's reign, French gentlemen wore wide-topped bucket boots. This fashion forced them to swing their legs as they walked, so that their toes turned outwards as their feet touched the ground. This style persisted even when the fashion for such boots died out.

You can see the same sort of rolling walk today in a fisherman wearing long waders, who has to circle his legs outwards as he strides.

Early court dance steps were intended mainly to show off the men's elegant turn of toe. Women dancers copied this style, and took part in what had earlier been a pastime for men. Some of the ballroom dances of

Bucket boots and boned dresses influenced early styles of dancing

that day were the *Passe-pied*, the *Sarabande* and the *Minuet*. The quick dances needed light, rhythmic footwork, and the slow ones controlled balance. Turn-out gave this control. As dance steps became more and more complicated, it was found that turn-out also gave the dancer strength and the ability to hold himself upright. The long, heavy costumes of the ladies, with their tight, boned bodices, made a straight back essential. Similarly, the men wore tight doublets.

Today's ballet dancer, trained in turn-out, has two-way stretch muscles. Standing on one leg, the other one can be raised at any angle to the body without disturbing the balance. If a dancer has naturally free-moving joints, this is a great asset, but training will help him or her to rotate the legs freely in the hip sockets, and make movement easier.

It was strict etiquette in Louis XIV's court that no one should turn his back on the king. This rule also affected the development of early ballet dancing. Courtiers danced not only for their own pleasure, but to entertain the king, who, when ill health forced him to stop dancing, designed ballets instead. So dances were often created to be seen from the front, as in a theatre, and it was found that turn-out gave the most pleasing line to the dancers' movements when viewed from the front.

The five positions of the feet

Strictly speaking, all movements in classical ballet are made with the feet and legs turned out as far as possible, and begin and end in one of the five positions of the feet. These five positions have been designed to help the dancer keep his or her balance, which takes years of practice. Even a professional dancer occasionally falls.

The pictures show the five positions a dancer aims to achieve. If you have never learned ballet, and try out these positions, you will find yourself using muscles you hardly knew were there. You will see just how difficult it is to hold your tummy in and your tail in when you are turning out your feet. But slowly this is managed, and the dancer learns to turn out her feet while keeping an upright posture.

Constant use of turn-out affects the way dancers walk.

First position of the feet in ballet

Second position; weight balanced evenly over feet

Third position is easier than fifth

Sometimes they are rudely teased for walking with their feet turned out like ducks.

There are two kinds of fifth position. In the easier one the front foot's heel is in line with the big toe joint of the back foot. When the whole front foot is aligned to the whole back foot a very strong turn-out has to be maintained, and this is really too difficult for a learner. A teacher has to guide and correct the dancer's balance as the position is attempted.

The dancer has to practise these positions constantly, so that his or her feet automatically use them as if there were no other way of moving. So often do the feet obey the brain, that these five positions become second nature to a trained dancer.

The dancer's feet A dancer's feet need to be flexible. Ballet exercises will strengthen them,

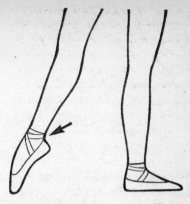

The Achilles tendon must be flexible

and also make the Achilles tendon pliant. A tendon is a cord of tissue forming the end of a muscle. The Achilles tendon is the tendon of the heel, by which the muscles of the calf of the leg are attached to the heel. When the instep is stretched the Achilles tendon contracts. Circle your foot and feel the action of the tendon as you do. It goes up your leg from the back of your foot.

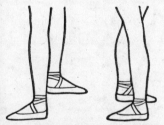

Fourth open (left) *and crossed, weight balanced evenly over feet*

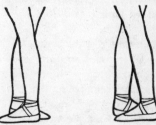

Two versions of fifth position, the more difficult on the right

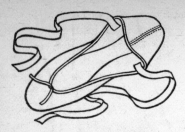

*A soft ballet shoe with ribbons
sewn in their correct position*

Ballet shoes Many teachers
advise their pupils when buying
ballet shoes, because their fit and
comfort is crucially important.
Choose shoes with care, and do
not be satisfied with a pair which
is slightly too small or too big.

Ballet shoes are made inside
out. When they have been
pleated, moulded on a last, and
the upper section sewn to the
leather sole, they are turned the
right way out. The leather of the
upper and the sole must be flexible,
for easy bending of the foot.

When you are stitching elastic
or ribbons to your shoes it is
important not to stitch through
the draw tape. If you do, the
tape cannot be drawn up
properly, to give the shoe a
snug fit. If you wear out a
ballet shoe, keep the inner sole
(the leather reinforcing the
instep). It can be re-used to
strengthen the shoes when they
soften. Satin shoes can be
cleaned by brushing them gently

with an old toothbrush dipped
in surgical spirit.

At first, pointe work was
carried out in shoes with no
stiffening. Today's dancers have
special shoes, with stiffening
along the sole and instep. The
dancer has to get used to this
thicker sole and must learn to
rest firmly on the papier-mâché
blocking in the toe of the shoe,
without wobbling.

*Fanny Bias on pointes in 1821.
Pointe shoes today have stiffened
toes, darned to lengthen their life*

Special pointe shoes were invented about a hundred and fifty years ago. They have become stronger and harder as more pointe work has been asked for in ballets, but they are still designed only for strong feet and not as an easy means for anyone to dance on their toes.

As the papier-mâché in the pointe shoe's toe softens and wears out quickly, most dancers darn the tip with heavy embroidery silk or carpet thread to prolong the shoe's life. You can use a large darning needle, or a curved upholstery one, which may be easier to handle. The darning also protects the satin of the toe and muffles the 'clonk' when a dancer lands on stage. Dancers are taught how to darn their shoes.

The correct fitting of shoe ribbons is most important. These are often partly lined with tape to strengthen them in case the silky ribbon tears, and to give firmer support. Again, a teacher will help. She will show a pupil where to sew on ribbons, first pinning them in place, and trying them out to see that the dancer's ankle and instep can move with complete freedom when they are tied. The shoe should be tied with your foot flat on the floor, and with the leg leaning backwards a little.

If you tie the ribbons with your foot bent this will hamper the movement of your ankle.

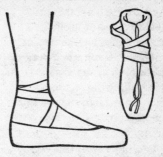

A correctly tied shoe. When not in use it should be folded as shown

Ribbons must fit smoothly round the foot and ankle, with no gaps or ends sticking out. Some dance companies have been known to make dancers pay a small fine if their ribbon ends show in a performance!

The dancer is also taught how to tie her two ribbons; they are passed across the top of the foot, round the back of the ankle and back to the front, lying one on top of the other. Then they are drawn to the back again, knotted twice, and the ends tucked into the slight hollow between the ankle and the Achilles tendon (see page 35). The knot should be on the outside of the leg, where it will not be rubbed undone when the feet and ankles brush against one another.

Sometimes, to make sure that these ends do not slip, the dancer moistens them with a little spit and rosin. This trick of the trade is also sometimes applied to the shoe itself. The dancer will moisten the heel of her tights with spit, then put on a little rosin, to keep the shoe from slipping off. Rosin is more usually rubbed into the soles of the shoes to reduce the risk of skidding.

Pointe shoes wear out very quickly if used continuously, and may only last for four or five days in a state fit for stage performance. A ballerina might use up two pairs of shoes, for instance, in one performance of *The Sleeping Beauty*. After that, they will be used in rehearsals for class until they fall to pieces. Each dancer will take great pains to make sure that her shoes are quite right, so that she will dance her best.

Pointe work Classical ballet is well known for the use of dancing on the tips of the toes – sur les pointes. (See page 17 for the early history of pointe work.) Occasionally male dancers have been required to dance on pointe, but generally this is a strictly female province.

The female dancers' muscles have to be prepared to support

Men rarely dance on pointes, but Bottom does in Ashton's The Dream

all her weight literally on her toes. Exercises will also work to strengthen weak ankles, so that the dancer can stand on pointe in perfect balance, without wobbling. The teacher will watch to see that the dancer is standing on pointe without leaning, curving the foot out forwards, or tilting it backwards. Properly fitting pointe shoes are essential, as a shoe which is too short or too long in the front can cause these faults. Ideally, a straight line could be drawn down through the centre of a foot which is properly balanced.

Sometimes the dancer has to rise slowly through *demi-pointe* on to pointes or lower herself slowly from pointes in the same way until her feet are flat on the floor again (see page 46). This slow rising is even harder than the quick kind of pointe work, where the dancer springs up lightly on to a foot which is completely stretched and returns through the foot equally quickly to the floor.

Proper training is needed to prepare a pupil for pointe work. If it is attempted before her muscles are strong enough, she may injure her feet, ankles or knees.

Most teachers agree that pointe work should not be attempted until a girl has been having regular lessons for at least two years and is at least ten years old. At a specialist school, those girls who have short, strong, 'square' looking feet may start on pointe at eleven, and often make quick progress, with ease. Those with weaker feet are introduced to pointe work more gradually.

These pictures of the five positions of the feet *sur les pointes* (on pointe) look very elegant, and show you what you will be able to do later on when your feet are ready.

A correct balance on pointe

The five positions on pointe, weight evenly balanced over feet

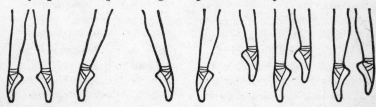

A flexible back is important for both male and female dancers

The legs and back A dancer's legs need to be straight and strong. In dancing the knees are either straight with pulled-up muscles, or bent and flexed deliberately. The back too should be straight, with the spine well held and the weight of the body evenly distributed over both feet. For bending, the back also needs to be supple. Twenty-five years ago or so, men were not expected to bend as far as girls, but now they do.

Although the dancer's feet and legs may seem all-important, in fact the dancer uses all her body. She is able to twist from her waist upwards, and this is called *épaulement* ('shouldering').

She may bend sideways, forwards or backwards, or she may just turn her shoulders slightly while moving gracefully. The least alteration in the way the shoulders are held can give a different appearance to a position of the body. It is rather like a change of expression in the speaking voice.

The arms and hands From the days of Louis XIV onwards, the arms were used to balance the dancer's body. At first, in tight court dresses, they were not raised above shoulder level. Gradually basic positions were formulated, as with the feet and legs. These are the starting and stopping places of arm movements, but they are not as strictly observed as the foot positions. In fact, it is simpler to give the French names for the main positions of the arms, and follow any numbering given as you are taught, because this varies from school to school and country to country. Epaulement gives arm positions endless variety too.

The main principle with the arms is that they must never show strain, even down to the tips of your little fingers. First, you need to stand properly. In what is sometimes called first position, a girl's little fingers should be held about ten centimetres in front of her thighs. If you imagine wearing a tutu, you would just miss touching it. A boy's little fingers would be held about five centimetres in front of his thighs.

If you look at pictures of dancers, you will see that there are many variants of these arm positions, and there are various *ports de bras* ('carriage of the arms') exercises to be practised. (See page 64 for a description of class exercises.)

The arms move sometimes along the same track, sometimes independently. It is helpful to watch your arm movements in a mirror. Your shoulders should always be kept down, without a suspicion of a hunch. The arms should move as freely from the shoulders as the legs do from the hip sockets, without disturbing the body. When raised above the head, the arms should not be held too far back, or the head will look poked forward. You should be able to glimpse the arms out of the corner of your eye.

The elbows should be held up, but not in a stiff 'corner'. This may at first make them ache. The wrists should also be held and not allowed to sag down or stick up. The fingers are held

gently together, with the thumb falling slightly inwards towards the palm of the hand.

You should aim for a graceful line from shoulder to fingertips. Some teachers suggest shutting your eyes for a while as you practise your arm movements. Then open your eyes, and check if you have arrived at the position you imagined, and if it is as good as you meant.

Arms are held gracefully, with no elbows or fingers sticking out

The head The movement of the head cannot be separated from that of the arms and shoulders. Pleasing movements are made when the head harmonises with the arms and they look good together. The eyes follow through what the arms are doing, and so they direct the head. Again, the ideal is to avoid stiffness or strain, and the head should move easily in conjunction with the rest of the body.

There are five main positions of the head, with many variations. Try them in a mirror, first without moving your shoulders and then with the shoulders moving a little in sympathy, whichever way seems most comfortable.

The positions of the head.

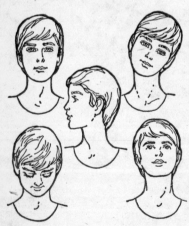

Three hairstyles for girl dancers

The hair The dancer's hair contributes so much to her appearance and elegance of line that it has to be given special consideration.

It is usually parted in the centre, to give the impression that any head movements are as well balanced as those of the arms and legs. If you secure short hair tightly in a net, or, if long, in a bun or plaits tied across the top of your head, your head will have freedom to move. Your teacher will be able to see exactly what your head and neck are doing, if there is no hair masking the nape of your neck.

A hairband will also help to secure fly-away hair, and give the smooth, neat head which is required in classical ballet. Boys sometimes wear sweat bands to

keep their hair out of the way.
Ballerinas may choose to wear
their hair over the ears and in a
low bun for romantic ballet,
and in long plaits or loose for
national dances. If your hair is
suitable, you can copy this.

The arabesque The *arabesque*
is a beautiful pose, and illustrates
perfectly the ideals of line and
balance in classical ballet.

The dancer stands on one leg,
and raises the other leg behind,
stretching it out straight. The

back should not sag, but should
be held comfortably, with the
leg raised only as high as the
dancer can keep it with graceful
ease. An *arabesque* will improve
as the dancer's technique does.

The dancer's arms match and
balance the line of her legs, and
are either both stretched out in
front, with one held higher than
the other, or one behind and one
in front. In whatever form the
arabesque is held, the arms should
not be tense, and the shoulders
should not feel strain. The arms
should follow a natural line from
the shoulders, with the head held
upright. The eyes follow the
hands, whose palms are turned
downwards; or sometimes the
dancer looks out towards the
audience.

*A beautiful, flowing arabesque -
one of the basic poses of ballet*

Positioning of the body The turn-out adopted in classical ballet has influenced the design of its positions and movements. (For turn-out, see page 33.) These are planned to be seen from the front, so from the audience's viewpoint the dancer's legs sometimes look 'crossed' (*croisé*) and sometimes 'open' (*ouvert* or *effacé*). The word *effacé* means 'shaded', and describes the effect of the arm or leg turned a little and shading part of the body. It is also used generally, for the positions when the feet are 'open'. Once again, there are variants, but the pictures show you some basic poses. When the legs are raised these poses become more striking still.

If the body is turned diagonally, or slanting from the audience's viewpoint, the position is *écarté*. This means 'separated' or 'wide apart'. Such a pose gives a wide view of the dancer. The head is turned sideways, to balance the appearance of the body. This stance is built on the 'open' feet of the second position (see the picture on page 34).

From left to right: the body posed in croisé, effacé *and* écarté

aid balance, and can be held in various positions. The dancer may look up at her hand or out at the audience.

Seven main movements have become the traditional ways in which a classical ballet dancer uses and links the positions and poses already described.

'Plier' ('to bend') Bending or flexing the knees is a part of many steps, as you can see after watching a few minutes of ballet. All jumps, for instance, begin and end with a *demi-plié* – a 'half-bend'. The 'full-bend' is called a *grand plié*.

The attitude - *a lovely pose*

The attitude This pose needs strength, and the pictures show the excellence for which you will be striving.

The dancer stands on one leg and raises the other leg behind or in front. The raised leg is bent into a right angle. When the pose is perfect, the raised thigh should be at right angles to the supporting thigh too. The arms, of course,

Plier

'Etendre' ('to stretch') The knees are stretched and extended after they have been bent in a *plié*, and the term *tendu* is also used when the foot is fully pointed, with the instep arched. Sometimes the term *dégagé* ('disengaged') is used when the foot slides from a closed position and stretches out into a open position forwards, sideways or backwards (see also *battement tendu*, page 57).

Etendre

'Relever' (to raise up again') This movement is carried out by the feet, as the dancer rises up on to the ball of the foot or the tips of the toes (see also pointe work, page 38). From flat on the floor (*à terre*), the foot moves to a position 'at quarter' (*à quart*), 'at half pointe' (*à demi*), at three-quarters' (*à trois quarts*) or 'on full pointe' (*sur les pointes*). As with pointe work, the foot may move smoothly, or with a little spring.

Relever

Sometimes you may also meet the term *chassé* ('chased'), which is also used in ballroom dancing. In ballet, this often describes the movement on one foot along the floor, forwards, backwards or sideways, from a *demi-plié* in fifth position to one in second or fourth position.

'Tourner' ('to turn') Dancers may turn on the balls of their feet or on their toes. They may swivel on their feet. They may jump up and turn in the air. The many variations are gradually taught in class.

'Glisser' ('to glide') Gliding movements by the feet contribute a great deal to the appearance of elegance and ease which marks good classical dancing.

'Elancer' ('to dart') This is a quick movement used for certain springy steps. The dancer may also dart on to the ball of the foot, or on to full pointe.

Glisser

'Sauter' or 'jeter' ('to jump')
The jumps in classical ballet are often performed most spectacularly by men. The dancer moves upwards from his heel through his foot and into the air. Then he lands, toes through to heel, in a *demi-plié*. *Jeter* literally means 'to throw', and is used for those steps when a dancer jumps off from one or both feet and lands on one or both feet. He may jump from one foot and land on the other foot. Movements upwards are described as having *élévation* ('elevation', 'being raised up').

Jeter

Music: a dancer's inspiration

The development of ballet has always been accompanied by a widening choice of music. At first, ballet was performed to the music of stately court dances. Now it is danced to every kind of music you can think of: mediaeval music; specially composed scores by Tchaikovsky, Stravinsky or Prokofiev; piano or harpsichord music; chamber music by Brahms; symphonic works, like Mahler's *Song of the Earth*; ragtime; jazz; even electronic music. (See page 87 for a list of ballet music to enjoy.) Sometimes ballet is even danced in silence.

Usually, however, ballet expresses something about music. The dancer interprets the music with his body, his limbs and his face. And he is helped by the rhythm he hears in the music, and by his imagination.

It is therefore crucial for a dancer to learn to listen to music. You cannot start too early. Rudolf Nureyev, who knew he wanted to be a dancer by the time he was eight, felt like a bird trapped in a net if he could not release his energy in dancing. But he spent hours of his childhood sitting absolutely still, listening to music on the radio.

You probably have access to a radio or a record-player and can teach yourself to concentrate on music. Listen carefully to pieces you enjoy so that no detail escapes you. Learn to 'know' the music, as if you were dancing to it and had to know the score bar by bar. It is well worth knowing at any point what is going to follow: a drum beat, a quick waltz or a relentless march.

Frederick Ashton has said that when he is composing a ballet he plays the music for it over and over again, and listens to no other music. Then he begins to think of steps, and goes to the studio and works them out with the dancers. He has done his homework before, and such preparation makes his job easier. In the same way, an ability to listen to music will make you a better dancer.

As the dancer hears the music, he responds with his steps in such a way that he passes on what he feels about the music to his audience. The choreographer has chosen what steps will express what he wants to say by means of dancing.

Of course, the interpretation of music can vary enormously. Sometimes music gains a new dimension for the audience when dancers express its beauty with their patterned movements. Sometimes dancers add a story to the music, and music and dancing combine to tell the story, acting out a plot and providing background and atmosphere too.

It is worth watching other dancers as you try to teach yourself to listen hard. When you are resting in class, look and see if they are really hearing the beat of the music or merely thinking of getting the steps right. Are they dancing *with* the music, or just *to* it?

In a small way, you can become a choreographer. You may be given the opportunity to make up your own dance to music in class, and you can practise at home too. If music suggests an atmosphere or a happening to you, try to express it by your steps and movements. You may find it easier to make up steps in your own room, or in front of a mirror, rather than plotting them on paper. But if you are including other dancers, you may find it easier to try out movements with markers or soldiers on a board first. When you have tried to invent your own dances and have managed to leave no gaps in the flow of movement, you will appreciate the skills of a good choreographer all the more.

Private practice may have to be done without music – then you will hear your thuds! But it is the dancer's musical response which transforms ballet from a series of planned movements accompanied by music to a performance worth watching. It is not brilliant physical jerks, but an art.

Margot Fonteyn has said, 'I take all my guidance from the music,' and that is good advice for all fledgling ballet dancers.

Mime: a dancer's acting

The art of mime is to tell a story or express a feeling or mood without using words. This is an extremely important part of a dancer's training.

The instruments at the dancer's command are every part of the body. Ballet training teaches the student to make controlled movements and rely on his head, body, arms, legs and feet to do exactly what he intends, so a dancer is well equipped to be good at the sign language of mime. And you will know from the outline of ballet's history given at the beginning of this book that there have been frequent attempts to make ballet more than just beautiful dancing of composed steps, but rather an entertainment which has something to 'say' to its audience.

You may have seen old silent films on television, where artists like Charlie Chaplin or Buster Keaton have acted out whole stories, with only a few words written on the screen. They have been able to make you laugh out loud by the comic use of their bodies, and the expressive use of their faces. You may also have seen on television or at first hand a conductor 'telling' his orchestra how to play, not only with his hands and a baton, but with the expressions on his face.

Today, there is a great interest in mime as an entertainment, and in 1978 Marcel Marceau, the French mime artist, opened an international school of mime in Paris, hoping eventually to build up a company. Christopher Bruce of the Ballet Rambert has collaborated with Lindsay Kemp, a mime, actor, dancer and teacher who has choreographed and produced his own works as well as some David Bowie pop concerts.

The skill of mime suits television and dramatic ballet very well. When dancers can act convincingly, it is possible to tell a dramatic story based on actual events. Kenneth Macmillan, an original member of the Sadler's Wells Theatre Ballet who has composed and directed many ballets, based his work *Mayerling* (1978) on a true story of the violent death of Crown Prince Rudolf and his lover in 1889. Mime is

Marcel Marceau - the greatest mime artist of our time

used to convey the idea of gunshot wounds and a hidden corpse. In contrast, Frederick Ashton has his dancers behaving as naturally as possible in a more gentle way in *A Month in the Country* (1976). He makes a joke of a prolonged search for a key. The son of the household bounces his ball to the music. Dancers make ordinary movements, like slumping into a chair, and walk off to the music so naturally that the audience almost expects to hear a murmur of conversation.

How mime came into classical ballet Mime has been an art form since Roman times. In the sixteenth and seventeenth centuries, mime companies travelled all over Europe, playing in the open air. The most famous were from Italy (the 'Commedia del Arte'), and included clowning, tumbling, songs and dances with their mime. Since it needed no words, this entertainment was understood wherever the players went, and an Italian company took over a theatre in Paris at the time ballet was developing at court. In 1708, a mimed play was given by two dancers from the Paris Opéra.

This helped to give French choreographers the idea that, in spite of its humble street background, mime could be brought even into aristocratic ballet, just as the skills of fairground acrobats had been. So passages of mime were used to link the dances in a ballet, where once songs had been used to tell the story.

By the nineteenth century, a formal language of mime had been adopted in ballet. In the full version (not always seen today) of the second act of *Swan Lake*, for instance, there are ten scenes, set to twenty-five minutes of Tchaikovsky's music. They consist of the huntsmen's mime with the prince; the swan queen's mime; the entry and dance of the swan maidens, the corps de ballet; their waltz; a grand pas-de-deux; the dance of the little swans; a dance by two swans; the swan queen's solo; a dance finale and a mime finale.

During this century, such formal mime has often been cut or changed, and in modern ballets it is incorporated into the steps and not acted out separately. So a character dancer will mime 'in character', just as the person he is portraying in dance would do. One outstanding character is the Widow Simone in *La Fille Mal Gardée* (The Unchaperoned Daughter), an old ballet revived in a new production by Frederick Ashton (1960). The widow is danced by a man, acting just like a pantomime dame.

From left to right: 'die', 'handsome man' and 'marry' in mime

Of course, facial expressions are always important and noticed particularly by audiences, but you will perhaps see the clearest examples of miming with the whole body in modern ballets. Expressiveness has become more important than beauty, and the dancers' bodies may be strangely contorted to convey misery or struggle or death.

Miming you can try for yourself If you attend weekly ballet lessons, and have done any suggested exercises at home, you may wonder what else you can do to make progress as an all-round dancer.

One thing is to practise mime, alone or with a friend. Dressing up may help you, even if you use only the simplest of bedspread cloaks, because it will be easier to assume a character if you *feel* like him or her. A long dress may help you to feel regal, a home-made teased-out string wig and hat more like a wicked witch. You will find movement different in a long skirt, jeans or shorts.

Any acting helps you develop two qualities you will need as a dancer. The first of these is imagination, to convince yourself and an audience that you are a princess or a dashing prince. You will have to think about how to do this, how to walk and stand, perhaps using a mirror.

The second quality is observation. If you are attempting to act as someone else, you must know how other people behave. You must watch them. It will make everyday life much more interesting to observe exactly how someone walks when tired, frowns when angry, cries when unhappy.

Working on these skills of imagining and watching, you can act out moods. If you have a friend to work with, you can take it in turns to guess what the other person is trying to show: fear, guilt, happiness, anger, greed, hunger, or (a hard one to do by yourself) jealousy.

You can also practise miming actions to your reflection in the mirror or to a critical friend who will tell you if she is convinced or not. Carrying things (light or heavy); lifting a baby or a sack of potatoes; doing routine jobs like cleaning; bicycling, running and walking in different ways can be tried out. Why not mime the walks of one person at seven, seventeen, twenty-seven and seventy-seven? Or together with a partner you can act out a sad farewell, a happy reunion, or a hectic quarrel.

In your first dance classes, you will probably have separate mime teaching. But all such practice will help you to interpret ballet. Then your audience will know just what the choreographer wanted to tell them in story or mood when he composed the ballet.

3 How is ballet learned?

Ballet class

Every ballet dancer goes to class. Even leading ballerinas go to a daily class throughout their dancing lives. The shape and purpose of a great company's dancing lesson is just the same as yours, even if some of the exercises and steps are more difficult. Anthony Dowell has said that every day he starts back at 'square one'. Every day the body has to be tuned up and prepared for the exertion of ballet dancing, so his class and yours is divided up into two main parts: barre work and centre practice.

Work at the barre Most dance studios have a wooden rail or rails fixed round the walls. The dancer holds this 'barre' to support him, and younger dancers use a lower barre. For practice at home a chairback is a good substitute. If you put too much pressure on it, both you and the chair will overbalance!

Barre exercises are done in the first part of class. They consist of broken down elements of the steps you will be doing in the centre of the room later on. The amount of time spent on them will vary, because the teacher has to decide what is needed by each particular set of pupils. Some teachers give more time to barre work because ballet today has become more acrobatic, with the elevation of the leg higher than it used to be, for example. To raise the leg higher needs more strength and control.

Acrobats can show how hard their tricks are – thrilling the audience and making them wonder, as circus drums roll, whether they will manage their amazing lifts and spins. Ballet dancers have to hide their strain. So the exercises which begin class enable dancers to work at strenuous movements until they *look* effortless.

You should not stretch and kick out hard before barre work, but warm up the body slowly, loosening the joints and getting the circulation going. If you are ready before class, you can start carefully, studying your own body and perhaps working facing the barre to avoid being distracted.

The aim of barre work after this warming up is to strengthen the muscles and practise control of the body, legs and feet. While you are working, the teacher will be watching, and will come and help you correct your posture. The importance of a straight back will often be mentioned, and the teacher will tell you to tuck in your tail and never look down at your feet, which must know their own way of working.

The head should also learn control, and the eyes should not stare, but look outwards to an imaginary audience, or follow the movement of the hand. As you work, the teacher may say: 'Lift yourself out of your body,' so that you feel slim and tall. She will choose exercises which suit your stage of development.

These are the exercises done at the barre in most ballet classes. Each exercise is done facing one way and then the other, so that both sides of the body are exercised equally. Some exercises may be done facing the barre.

Pliés (bends – see also page 45) These full and half bends of the knees are the first exercises done in class, and warm up the leg muscles. They help the dancer to

Grand plié

turn out (see page 33) and to balance the body evenly over both feet. Beginners will do *pliés* in the first, second and third positions; later on, the fourth and fifth positions will be used too. These movements should be smooth, and the dancer should

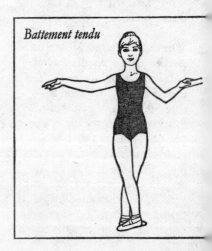

Battement tendu

56

take as long to bend low in *grand plié* till his thighs are parallel with the floor as he does to rise again to straightened legs.

The word *battement* means 'a beating of the leg or foot'. There are several beats in ballet.

Battement tendu (stretched) Starting in first or fifth position, the working foot slides out forwards, backwards or sideways to a fully arched position, and then returns to first or fifth. The aim of this exercise is to strengthen the instep.

Battement dégagé

Battement dégagé (disengaged) or *glissé* (gliding) These movements are the same as those of the *battement tendu*, except that the foot is 'disengaged' or raised just a little from the floor in its fully arched position. The movements are quick and prepare the dancer for speedy footwork.

Battement fondu (melting) This exercise is for smooth bending of the supporting knee, and prepares the dancer for taking off and landing when jumping.

Battement frappé (knocked) Another exercise to prepare the knee and foot for jumping, this

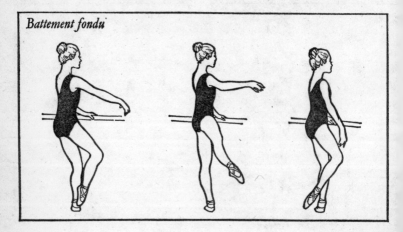

Battement fondu

will help strengthen your instep and thigh muscles. The knee of the working leg is bent and the working foot raised from fifth to a relaxed position either in front of, or behind the supporting ankle. It then moves out crisply, forwards, sideways or back, to a fully stretched position, the ball of the foot striking the floor in passing, and returns to the ankle. When fully stretched out the toes are just off the floor.

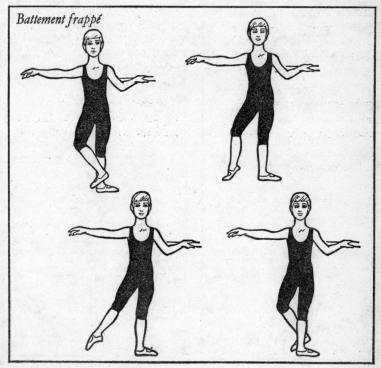

Battement frappé

Petit battement

Petit battement sur le cou du pied
(a little beat on the ankle)
Another exercise to prepare the
dancer for jumps and beats.
The working foot starts from the
same position as in *battement
frappé*. The upper leg is held
completely still, and the working
foot performs a series of rapid
movements from front to back
(or back to front) of the
supporting ankle.

Battement en cloche (like a swinging
bell) Both legs are kept straight
in this movement. The working
leg swings up forwards then
backwards, as high as the
student can comfortably manage
in a pendulum movement. This
is also called *battement balancé*,
and it should be a balanced
rocking from front to back, or
back to front at fourth position,
passing through first.

Battement en cloche

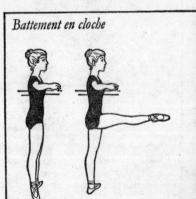

Grand battement

Grand battement (large) This 'big beating' develops control of the whole leg. The working leg is raised forwards, backwards or sideways to hip height or higher, starting and finishing in fifth. Remember to keep your weight over your supporting leg. You may have to do this exercise in the centre later, without the barre to steady you! Do not raise the hip of your working leg or twist your body.

Rond de jambe à terre et en l'air (a circling of the leg either touching the ground or raised) This movement actually makes an oval as the leg rotates in the hip socket. It helps the knee joints become more flexible. When the exercise is started, it may be done in four slow stages. The working leg should move smoothly.

Adage (slow moving) In these exercises the legs move slowly with perfect control. They help to strengthen the back.

One such exercise is *développé*, an 'unfolding' movement of the leg. The student should not try to lift the working leg too high, and should aim to look at ease, not contorted.

Rond de jambe

Développé

Centre practice Most dance studios have large mirrors on one or more walls, and in centre practice the student will be able to correct any movement or pose which does not look graceful. Leotards are worn so that the dancer's arms and legs are clearly visible. The students space themselves out so that they can see the teacher and the mirror, and be seen. Often the 'rows' are changed between exercises so that nobody is lurking at the back. In fact, you will be expected to *want* to be

63

Port de bras

seen at the front. Ballet is for performance, after all!

Port de bras (carriage of the arms) Exercises for the arms aim for flowing movements with no jerks or badly held fingers, wrists or elbows.

The positions of the arms are described on page 40. Port de bras exercises consist of a series of movements through these positions. You might, for example, start with your arms held low (*en bas*), lift them in front of you (*en avant*), open them out (*sur le côté*) and lower them (*en bas*) again.

Sometimes each arm is exercised separately. In more advanced work, they will move in different tracks, at different paces.

Adage Some of the slow exercises you have done at the barre will be repeated in the centre *sur place* (on the spot), balancing your body without support. In centre practice you learn to change your weight from one foot to another, and to move smoothly in different directions.

Temps lié (linked time) There are various forms of this exercise, which prepares the body for moving in a series of steps. A simple version is illustrated here.

Temps lié

The teacher may call out or demonstrate several steps which together make a sequence or *enchaînement*, and the class then dances them. This tests the student's ability to fit steps to music, and to remember their order. Sometimes you may be given a chance to invent your own series of steps. In this part of the lesson you may also practise the beautiful poses, *arabesques* and *attitudes* (see the pictures on pages 43-5).

Pas de bourrée (bourrée steps) These little steps are used to link movements. The feet are in fifth position on demi pointe or full pointe, and the dancer changes weight quickly from foot to foot while moving across the floor. These steps take their name from an old French dance.

Pas de bourrée

Allegro (lively) This is the name for quicker steps and exercises, and in particular jumps (see page 48 *sauter* or *jeter*). Jumps are very important for boys and should have a prominent part in the lesson.

Jumps start and finish in *demi-plié*. For small jumps, the impetus is from the feet, but when you jump higher the strength will also come from your thigh and bottom muscles. You must take care not to stick out your bottom or chest and spoil the poise of the top of your body.

When a dancer can control his jumps, he will appear to hover in the air before sinking back into a *demi-plié*. This bouncing rise, achieved only after much hard work, is called *ballon* (a ball). Landing incorrectly can damage the knees. Now the dancer learns the value of all the *plié* exercises done earlier in class. In jumping the arms should be kept under control and not allowed to flap about. The great Russian dancer, Nijinsky (see page 21), used to astound audiences with his jumping.

Tours en l'air (turns in the air) In these a dancer turns as he jumps. A professional male dancer has to be able to do a double turn, but that is a long way ahead of you!

A jump

Pirouette

Pirouettes (turns) *Pirouettes*, however, may well come into your lessons. These are turns in which the dancer spins round on one leg. They can be in *adage* or *allegro* versions. As the feet grow stronger, the supporting foot will rise from quarter to half to three-quarter pointe, now commonly used by boys as well as girls. And, when ready, girls will spin on pointe.

Pirouettes can be done on the spot, or travelling round the studio or diagonally from corner to corner. You will first learn them on the spot. To avoid dizziness, the dancer focuses her eyes on a spot in front. She starts to turn her body but keeps watching the same spot, flicking her head round to the front at the last moment as she completes the turn. Beginners may attempt the *pirouette* in four separate quarter turns to get the idea of this head movement.

No written account of ballet steps and exercises can replace a teacher who shows and tells you exactly what to dance and how, but some understanding of how your body is being trained may help you to work better. And all the hard work will seem worthwhile to hear her call out 'Good!' as you dance across the studio floor.

Your classical ballet lessons are the foundation of your dancing technique, but you may find that your talents are best shown in 'character' dance. You can take separate 'character' classes to learn pieces which are often national or folk dances in origin. Some may be comic or dramatic, and give you a chance to act as you dance in character. Or you may take 'modern' classes, which teach dance styles used in musicals and experimental ballet theatre today.

One teacher who had been teaching ballet for forty years said that only four of the pupils she had taught over that period had entered classical ballet companies, although many had become dancing teachers. Few of the thousands of young people taking ballet lessons today become professional dancers, and anyone who has ever studied ballet knows how much less easy it is than it appears.

However, if you persist with your classes you will be rewarded by learning more about how ballet is made, and what good dancing is like. Your own strength and grace will increase. And, most important, you will enjoy dancing for the pleasure of moving to music.

Ballet school

The first thing ballet students learn is to work hard. If you enter a specialist school of any kind, you will be facing an intensive course. If the school is a ballet school, pupils will be quick to tell you that the work is hard because it needs their full concentration. If you have taken ballet classes you will understand this, because dancing needs not only physical effort, but mental effort, to think about what you are doing and why.

A specialist dancer aims to do his best every day, to improve and maintain an improvement, and not to slip back. He is on show in class. A serious student studies his own weaknesses and tries to cure them by perseverence. High standards are expected by all teachers, because their classes are picked from many people seeking places. Students know they are lucky to be chosen.

How you enter ballet school A series of auditions is held every year for entry to ballet schools, some of which are boarding schools, for boys and girls from eleven to sixteen. Junior associate classes for children from eight to eleven are organised too. It is possible to work out what a child's fully grown height is likely to be, and a dancer will need to be well-formed, not too tall, healthy and strong. Schools sometimes ask to see photographs in leotards or trunks with the child's application form. Some applicants will already have taken exams set by the Royal Academy of Dancing. Girls, in particular, often start some sort of dancing lessons early, at five or so. They will be chosen for ballet school if they show promise – if they can work well, respond to music, and have the right sort of basic training, which has loosened them up and prepared them for concentrated dancing.

Boys can start later, up to the age of fourteen if they are loose-limbed and have the right sort of body to work at ballet. The Russian dancer Mikhail Baryshnikov did not enter ballet school in Riga until he was twelve, but he had been to a gymnastic school and played football before then. Even today, people do not always appreciate that it is very hard physical work to be a ballet dancer. The fame of such dancers as Rudolf Nureyev, Anthony Dowell and Mikhail Baryshnikov has helped to persuade the public that ballet dancing is as physically testing as athletics.

Obviously, dancing is the most important item on the time-table in ballet schools, but the schools want to produce intelligent, educated people, so a good general education is vital. Not all students will be able to stay in ballet, and they need a general education to prepare them for further training or jobs.

Stage schools may offer ballet as a special subject and also give time to tap and jazz and popular modern dancing. Some students specialise in drama too and work at mime and improvisation. Ballet and modern dance exams are taken.

Ballet schools naturally pay close attention to music, and many boys and girls learn to play instruments such as piano, flute, guitar and violin. Art is also given a good place in the time-table, as it relates to stage performance too. There is a lot to fit into a week, and days are demanding.

Subjects studied There is a daily ballet class, lasting about an hour and a quarter. Boys and girls work separately, except for character national dances; and at about fifteen they may start pas-de-deux classes together. Both boys and girls may do Scottish dancing and boys Morris dancing. Some students have one or two private coaching lessons a week, to improve, for instance, pointe work. They are expected to practise on their own or in pairs to improve shortcomings. Some take classes in choreography from the age of twelve onwards. They are taught history of the ballet too.

Swimming is considered good exercise for dancers. Some students play football, cricket, basket-ball and tennis. Others take fencing. Gym is often compulsory for younger pupils, and some boys do weight-lifting. Older students are able to give more time to dancing as their strength increases, and these other activities become second in priority. Most schools have classes on Saturday till midday, and Sundays are free.

General subjects are studied, and most students try for five or more 'O' levels, chosen from English, Maths, Religious Knowledge, French, possibly General Science, Civics, History, Music and Art. There may not be time for the other subjects available at ordinary schools, such as technical drawing or commerce.

Performances Part of the training at ballet school is for performing to an audience. Some schools give an annual production to the public,

The role of Clara in The Nutcracker *is always danced by a child*

and hours are spent on rehearsals. A programme for parents and friends might include short ballets created by students and their teachers. An English stick dance, a Scottish sword dance, a Sailors' Hornpipe, Edwardian ragtime dances and American square dances would show how versatile the ballet school students are. Part time pupils, working out of school, also put on displays. Some ballet school children may take small parts in Christmas shows such as *Nutcracker*, learning to project what talent they have to an audience. They will perform to each other and practise choreography, preparing ballets of increasing length as their skills develop. There may be chances to perform outside school in small groups or to dance on television.

Whenever possible, students are given the opportunity of seeing ballet live or on film, and of attending rehearsals to see a company prepare works for performance.

Boys' classes Even today ballet is less popular with boys than with girls and big classes for them are only likely to be found in specialist ballet schools. They have a better chance of future success than girls, as they face less competition for places in companies.

Boys' training emphasises strength and elevation. Classes are small, and good students are expected to correct themselves if they make a mistake. All through the long class they are listening, thinking and trying to make their bodies do what the teacher wants.

Students' attitudes to school At the end of class the dancers perform a *révérence* – a bow or curtsey – to their teacher and the hard-working pianist who has accompanied them. This is a mark of gratitude and a symbol of the students' desire to learn and pleasure in being taught. Even after working themselves to exhaustion and possibly being shouted at, almost bullied, students always say 'thank you'.

Learning ballet is not like learning an ordinary subject, and sometimes students in ballet schools feel set apart. They feel isolated, because their life is different, and because other people often regard dancing as an easy option, not a strenuous discipline.

The atmosphere inside ballet school is absorbed and enthusiastic and students always attend class promptly and properly dressed. Each student works away constantly to improve her dancing and satisfy her own standards. The teacher will help, but the student knows for herself if she is doing well.

All the hard work is worth it if an audience seems pleased to watch a student. She enjoys the atmosphere and feeling of satisfaction, and each public performance makes her more determined to become a professional dancer. Nothing would please as much, however testing the work behind the scenes. At this stage of her life, anything else seems second best.

Next steps towards ballet

At sixteen, ballet dancers enter a life which is more like student life at eighteen in other subjects. Those who have been lucky enough to attend junior ballet school have been well prepared for hard work, discipline and fierce competition. The next step is into the world of ballet.

Classes teach dancers to accept criticism of what they do without resentment, to try and act on it at once and to believe that obeying their teacher will improve their dancing. The excellent teachers who have also taught dancers to criticise themselves and to work out their own faults will now be appreciated by students applying to senior schools and companies. For when you are performing you have to criticise and correct yourself as you dance.

In a senior or upper school, a student may study for one or two 'A' levels, perhaps in English, French or History of Drama, but dancing comes first. Some boys and girls decide at this stage to take the three-year teachers' training course and give up ideas of becoming performers. For this they need five 'O' levels. Most students realise that they may have to consider teaching later on to earn a living, but at this stage want to try to enter a company at home or abroad. Those are the dancers who have found performing supremely enjoyable. They feel that they are achieving something by dancing to an audience. Students attend upper school for one, two or three years, because they may at any time be taken into a company. All depends on how a dancer works and develops. Talent will be noticed.

Some companies audition and accept dancers at sixteen and train them, but not in a formal school. Gradually, as dancers are ready, opportunities are given to perform. Because companies have different styles and repertories, the dancer who knows her own strengths will have an advantage. She will apply to an experimental, modern company, if that is her best style. She may hope to do choreography, and apply to a company which specialises in preparing new works. The director may be a choreographer she admires, and with whom she would like to work in order to learn from him. Touring companies lead a particularly strenuous life, but give wide experience in coping with different roles, with different stages and casts and tiring journeying, which must not be allowed to spoil performances.

When the company is at work, days have a routine of class, rehearsal, performance, and all the dancers' lives are geared to this rhythm. Operas may sometimes need dancers, who will then be working with singers as well as an orchestra. Some dancers take their talents into acting, and only occasionally dance on stage, but constantly display their ability to move well.

'Writing' and 'reading' ballet

From the history of ballet (see page 10), you will know that ballets used to be handed down from teachers to pupils and that choreographers relied on dancers' memories and any notes taken in rehearsal. Often dancers have come out of retirement to show how ballets were first performed. This had some advantages, but there remained a feeling that it should be possible to find a system of writing down dances. There have been many attempts. One system, invented in 1925 and called Labanotation, is still frequently used by modern dance groups.

Then, in 1947, Rudolph and Joan Benesh began to think of a way to write down a dancer's movements in classical ballet. They based their notation on that of music, and wrote it on the five-line stave used for music. Like music, ballet has rhythm and time to express, but the dancer's position must also be recorded. The Benesh system puts a human figure into a square, with the span of the arms equal to the height of the body.

Lines are used to mark the positions of the hands and feet, and they imply what the rest of the body is doing, in outline. Once the idea is mastered, there is no need to draw in the square.

If the hand or foot is level with the body, the sign is ▬. If either is in front of the body the sign is ▮, and if behind, this sign is used ●. Bending is marked by crosses, and movements by curved lines. There are, of course, many details to learn.

Benesh notation has become an invaluable shorthand of dancing, which some children study at ballet school. With this system new ballets can be learned ahead of practice, and older ballets brought to life.

Benesh notation is used today by some ballet companies in England, Scotland, Turkey, Holland, Germany, Canada, New Zealand, Australia, Norway and South Africa. Future members of such companies will be expected to read notation with ease.

As a result, a new job is now available in ballet – that of a notator or choreologist. This person makes a written record of the dance the choreographer invents. A fascinating development of notation has been its use in the field of medicine to record the movements of spastic children and thereby guide doctors and nurses in their treatment.

Teaching ballet

Some people have the gift of being able to pass on enthusiasm and bring out the talent in others. Ballet needs inspiring teachers, because so much is taught by demonstration and encouragement in class. You may decide that you would be better at teaching than at dancing yourself. When qualified, you can teach children and introduce them to the pleasures of ballet.

Famous teachers from the past are often remembered for their eccentric ways. One would rap dancers' feet and legs with his walking stick if they made mistakes. Another would provide music only by tapping with his cane and whistling. Some demonstrated every step. Others directed whole classes from the piano, improvising the music. Some teachers would shout with rage; others never lost patience, or even raised their voices. Each would have a special subject for concern. One would decide that correct breathing improves any movement; another would concentrate on care of the feet, and insist on dancers going home after class in boots, not shoes, to support their tired ankles (something you could try out).

To become a good teacher, you do not have to be odd, or fierce, but you do have to be able to draw out from your pupils the very best dancing they can do. You need the authority which comes from understanding dancing and how it is done. As each pupil is different, you will have to work with each as an individual. If you are good at observing, you can correct, help and encourage your students' dancing as it develops. Their progress will be your reward.

Often dancers turn to teaching when they are older, and bring their experience of stage performance when they coach new dancers. Dame Ninette de Valois' career has seen her as dancer, choreographer, producer, director and founder of a school and company – an extraordinary achievement for one person.

Ballerinas are sometimes invited to direct ballets in which they have danced for companies abroad, to whom the works are new. Georgina Parkinson, who has danced for nearly twenty years with the Royal Ballet, was asked to coach the American Ballet Theatre dancers in classical ballets. Lynne Seymour has become Director of the Munich Ballet Company. Beryl Grey, retired from dancing herself, is the Artistic Director of the London Festival Ballet. Dancers take up new rôles all their working lives. What seems clear is that a passion for dancing has rightly been compared with a disease. The only 'cure' is to dance, or to help others to dance.

4 What can you see at the ballet?

Classical ballet

If you are taking ballet lessons you will probably hope to see some classical ballets, to admire the dancing of those who have mastered the skills to which you are being introduced. You can appreciate the dancers' talent and work more because you know how hard it is to achieve lightness, beautiful line, and an interpretation of the music, all by given steps, which have to be remembered. The ballerina has so much to do, but must never look flustered or tired.

Classical ballets like *Nutcracker*, *Swan Lake* and *The Sleeping Beauty* are worth seeing more than once, to compare different performances. Perhaps such ballets, which tell a story, are the easiest to enjoy first. You can try *La Boutique Fantasque* (The Magic Toyshop), *La Fille Mal Gardée* (The Unchaperoned Daughter), *Coppélia*, *Giselle* and *The Dream*. All these tell stories in dance, and there are books which re-tell the stories of ballets for you to enjoy too (see page 85).

Giselle - *one of the best loved classical ballets*

Then there are ballets to watch simply for the pleasure of the dancing. They are abstract, and do not tell a story. *Les Sylphides*, to Chopin's music, and *Symphonic Variations*, to the Symphonic Variations for Piano and Orchestra by César Franck, are good examples. In contrast, *Elite Syncopations* is a suite of amusing dances to ragtime music.

Experiments in staging and costumes

The earliest ballets were spectacles, and up to this century beautiful costumes and scenery were essential to the pleasure audiences had when visiting the ballet. Artists were specially commissioned to paint suitable sets and a lot of money was spent on elaborate costumes. You can see pictures of early productions and classical revivals, and many ballets today still have marvellous sets and gorgeous costumes.

The other extreme, which you can see in some ballets today, is the use of a bare stage and shifting lighting. Dancers' costumes are simplified to robes, shifts or body tights. Small groups obviously find this economic, and could not afford to make large sets and transport them on tour, but this simplicity is deliberate. If a ballet can be freed from all the 'trimmings', it then has to stand on the merits of the choreography. The dancers reveal only their bodies, unembellished and uncluttered by even the most beautiful of costumes.

Experiments in dance

Modern dance has tried to free ballet from its own classical form, and paid most attention to expressing feeling and meaning. Choreographers have made steps which aim to convey emotion. Antony Tudor tried this in a dramatic piece called *Dark Elergies* as early as 1937, and Christopher Bruce's *Ancient Voices of Children* (1975) acts out the games and lives of poor neglected children.

Modern experiments have taken ballet steps further, making dancers adopt new positions and attitudes and contort their bodies in ways they did not know they could. Movements may include rolling on the floor or wrestling. The dancer becomes a pliable instrument for the choreographer to use.

For someone studying modern dance there is the excitement of experiment while learning. The student is taught how the body moves, improves his or her technique and then uses this knowledge. It may appeal to you to use your imagination to create new movements. Some modern classes allow time for pupils to try out their own moves.

Dancers taking part in contemporary works see the experiments taking place. It is impossible to do more than outline some of the strange ideas which have been made into dances in the name of ballet. Audiences vary in their reactions to these experiments: one man stood up in a Dance Festival, and shouted as he left the theatre: 'This is rubbish!' while another member of the audience answered: 'Go on. I love it!' You will have to make up your own mind which dance experiments impress you.

In one twenty-minute ballet two male dancers (one of them Rudolph Nureyev) in simple body tights dance to a song cycle, without a set or plot, and with only their own movements to capture the interest of the audience. Maurice Béjart (born in Belgium in 1927) devised this ballet, which was successful even in a giant arena holding nearly six thousand people.

A stark modern ballet devised by Maurice Béjart

These dancers had only the support of the music, but some ballets have tried movement without music. Jerome Robbins created *Moves, a Dance in Silence* in 1959, in which only the sounds of dancers' moving bodies were heard. Others have copied this idea. A lack of music removes one of the delights of ballet. It also takes away one of the aids to the dancer's memory, and so either the steps will have to be simplified or they may be allowed to become haphazard. Such experiments can be hard for an audience to understand.

Musical instruments have sometimes dominated modern ballets. For instance, in *Frames, Pulse and Interruptions*, created for the Ballet Rambert by the Dutch choreographer, Jaap Flier, and the composer, Harrison Birtwistle, the musicians are on the stage. Three bass trombone players and two amplified double basses face the audience, at the back of the stage. Four percussionists also play – one at each corner of the stage. The tempo of the music, and therefore the dancing too, is controlled by the beat of a drummer. It becomes a complicated game for dancers and players.

Modern dance is not always solemn. One ballet has all the company coming on stage in clownish overalls, climbing down from balconies in the theatre and rioting through the audience to dance mocking versions of well known dances in the classics and musicals.

Movements in modern dance may look jerky and fragmented. The dancers leap, or stand on one leg. They twist their bodies into peculiar shapes, and find new ways of supporting each other – not just the male dancer lifting the ballerina, as in classical ballet. One dancer lies on the ground on her side, with her neck resting on another dancer's instep. He lifts his foot slowly, and brings her to a half upright position. One dancer lies across the other's back. They dance separately or in disconnected groups. One dancer repeats the same action throughout a whole section of a ballet on the spot, while others move away, dancing the same action. Even painting becomes dance in one ballet, where a dancer lies on a large sheet of paper while another dancer draws round him. He moves his arms. When the new positions are drawn in, a many-armed creature appears. Experiments are seldom as odd as that, but they do seem a long way from ballet at times, and nearer to mime and gymnastics.

It is most often small groups who try out new productions, and they give their members chances to create ballets in workshops. It is worth going to see such experiments, which might inspire you to try choreography for yourself.

Influences on modern ballet

Other forms of dancing may interest you too. The precision of tap
dancing has fascinated many ballet dancers. They can see how it has
been influenced by jazz and African tribal dancing. Those who know
Lancashire clog dancing also see similarities in tap.

Disco dancing shows the strong influence of American Negro
dancing in many of the styles and steps which come and go in
popularity. Many ideas have been absorbed into modern ballet.
Aboriginal dances have been included in Australian dance festivals.
Primitive Negro dances have infiltrated into ballet, just as jazz has
coloured twentieth century music.

Dancing borrows from all around it. Dancers and choreographers
live in a changing world, and take into their ballets influences from
folk dancing at home and abroad. Travelling dancers may get a
chance to see the many Japanese ballet companies, or Balinese
dancing to gongs and drums, with the dancers sometimes playing the
instruments.

Television is becoming more adventurous in presenting ballet,
either filmed straight from stage performances or specially designed
for the small screen. The cinema also gives you the chance to see
foreign ballets and dancers of all kinds.

At its worst, modern dancing looks like meaningless exercises. At its best, modern dancing is full of new, stimulating ideas for movement with music.

Ballet all around you

If you are interested in ballet, it will spill over into all the dancing you can see and try out for yourself. But you will also be reminded of ballet's beauty and strength in surprising places.

Footballers have been known to attend ballet classes, to improve their balance. The poise of a high-jumper may remind us of dancers. The Royal Academy of Dancing has worked with coaches of the Amateur Athletic Association. High-jumpers and hurdlers have found special ballet exercises useful in their training.

Skate-boarding has its own style and grace, while ice-skating deliberately aims for beauty and balance, like ballet. John Curry, who always wanted to be a dancer, became world champion of ice-skating. But he also attends ballet classes, and has set up a school in New York. Trying to combine ballet with skating, he has presented 'Ice Dancing'. For these performances of dancing on ice, he has turned for help to ballet choreographers like Kenneth Macmillan.

Certainly, the amazing strength and balance of gymnasts brings modern ballet to mind, because it has become more obviously athletic than classical dancing.

You may enjoy dancing as a pupil, as a performer, or as part of an audience. As a ballet enthusiast, you have learnt about the dedication which produces excellent dancing. You understand why dancers would hate to give up dancing. The more you find out, by dancing or watching, the more you will be able to take delight in the enchanting, fascinating world of ballet.

Reading about ballet

A short list of books

CLARKE, Mary and CRISP, Clement: *Making a Ballet* (Studio Vista, 1974). Two of the articles in this older book are especially interesting: 'The Choreographer at Work', and 'The Dancer's Contribution'.

CLARKE, Mary and VAUGHAN, David (editors): *The Encyclopedia of Dance and Ballet* (Pitman Publishing, 1977). Not only classical but contemporary dance is recorded and illustrated.

DAVIS, Jesse: *Classics of the Royal Ballet* (Macdonald and Jane's, 1978). Full descriptions and excellent photographs of *Nutcracker, Swan Lake, La Fille Mal Gardée, Giselle, Romeo and Juliet* and *Sleeping Beauty*.

FONTEYN, Margot: *A Dancer's World* (W. H. Allen, 1978). For older readers, this account will hold much interest.

FRANKS, A. H. (editor): *Every Child's Book of Dance and Ballet* (Burke, 1957, revised 1973). A collection of articles. Full descriptions and music are given for two mimed dances, two ballet dances and two national character dances.

GLASSTONE, Richard: *Better Ballet* (Kaye and Ward, 1977). This is a beautifully illustrated and clear explanation of the principles of classical ballet. The book would help you to understand what you are taught in class.

GREGORY, John: *Understanding Ballet* (Octopus Books, 1972). This is a good book for studying pictures of dancers.

JESSEL, Camilla: *Life at the Royal Ballet School* (Methuen, 1979). There are three hundred new photographs in this book, which portrays the actual process of becoming a dancer, and explains how it is done.

KOEGLER, Horst: *The Concise Oxford Dictionary of Ballet* (OUP, 1977). Easy to use, clear definitions and accounts of dancers, their lives and work.

LAWSON, Joan: *Ballet Stories* (Ward Lock, 1978). Some stories from ballet are told and background details given; fully illustrated.

LAWSON, Joan: *Beginning Ballet, From the Classroom to the Stage* (A. & C. Black, 1977). Some helpful diagrams of exercises, and a useful section on making stage costumes of all kinds, including a basic leotard, the tutu, crossover and national costumes.

LEMAITRE, Odon-Jérôme with CHAUVIRÉ, Yvette: *Your First Book of Ballet* (Angus & Robertson, 1976). An attractively presented book, with some good material on choreographers, and a useful list of schools.

RICHARDSON, Jean: *Enjoying Ballet* (Hamlyn, Beaver original, 1977). This book tells a great deal about ballet dancers, ballets and how to enjoy visits to see ballet.

STREATFEILD, Noel: *A Young Person's Guide to Ballet* (Warne, 1975). An attractive and interesting account of the progress of a boy and girl who start dancing at nine, and learn a lot about ballet, its history and challenges in the three years of their lives which Noel Streatfeild's characteristic story-telling covers.

TERRY, Walter: *Ballet Guide* (David and Charles, 1976). Descriptions of more than five hundred major ballets of the world; illustrated.

Nonsuch in Education This company teaches and demonstrates the history of dance, in lectures, courses and workshops. Nonsuch (History and Dance) Limited, 16 Brook Drive, London SE11 4TT (Tel. 01 735 8353).

Listening to ballet

A short list of music

As records and tapes are frequently issued and deleted, it is best to go to a record dealer to find out what recordings are available. All these pieces have excellent recordings, and you may find a choice. Many libraries now have records, and this popular music would easily be found in second-hand shops too.

ADAM: *Giselle*

BERNSTEIN: *Fancy Free*

BORODIN: *The Polovtsian Dances from 'Prince Igor'*

CHOPIN: *Les Sylphides*

COPLAND: *Appalachian Spring* and *Rodeo*

DEBUSSY: *Prelude à l'Après-midi d'un Faune*

DE FALLA: *Ritual Fire Dance from 'Love the Magician'* and *The Three-cornered Hat*

DELIBES: *Coppélia*

OFFENBACH: *Barcarolle*

PROKOFIEV: *Romeo and Juliet*

RAVEL: *Bolero*

RIMSKY KORSAKOV: *Schéhérazade*

ROSSINI: *La Boutique Fantasque*

SCHUMANN: *Carnaval*

STRAVINSKY: *Firebird* and *Petrouchka*

TCHAIKOVSKY: *The Nutcracker, The Sleeping Beauty* and *Swan Lake*

WALTON: *Façade*

WEBER: *Invitation à la Valse*

Glossary

adage movement or dance in slow time.

allegro lively or fast movement.

arabesque a pose in which the dancer stands on one leg, and raises the other leg behind her, stretching it out straight.

assembler to bring together, referring to the feet.

à terre on the ground.

attitude a pose in which the dancer stands on one leg, while the other is held raised in front or behind her and bent at the knee.

balancer to rock or swing the leg.

ballon the rising bounce of a dancer into the air and ability to land lightly.

barre the wooden support rail on the walls of a dance studio.

battement beating, usually of the foot or leg.

battu beaten

bourrée an old French dance.

character (dancer) non-classical, national character (dancer).

chassé gliding movement of the foot.

choreographer someone who works out the sequences of dance movements in a ballet.

choreologist someone who writes down the dancers' movements in a ballet.

coupé cut.

croisé crossed.

de côté to the side.

dégager to disengage.

demi half.

derrière behind.

deuxième second.

devant in front.

développer to unfold the legs.

écarté separated.

effacé open, not crossed.

élancer to dart.

élévation rising in a jumping movement.

en arrière backwards.

en avant forwards.

en bas below.

enchaînement a set of linked steps.

en cloche like a swinging bell.

en dedans inwards.

en dehors outwards.

en face opposite.

en haut above.

en l'air raised, in the air.

entrechat crossing and beating of the feet during a jump.

épaulement the movement of the shoulders.

étendre to stretch.

exercices à la barre exercises holding on to the barre, which begin each class.

exercices au milieu centre practice, away from the barre.

fondu melting (of a movement).

frapper to strike.

glisser to glide.

grand big.

jeter to spring or jump.

leotard a sleeved or sleeveless costume for dancing, shaped like a swimsuit.

mime acting without speaking; showing character and meaning in actions, not words.

modern dance a free dance, not based on traditional classical ballet movements.

notation a written-down record of ballet or dance.

ouvert open, not crossed.

pas a step.

pas de deux a dance for two people.

penché leaning.

petit little, small.

piqué pricked; this usually describes a movement in which the dancer steps forward sharply on to pointe.

pirouette a spin of the body, balanced on the toes of one foot.

plier to bend.

pointe work dancing balanced on the tips of the toes, supported by blocks in the shoes.

port de bras the movements and carriage of the arms.

posé poised or balanced; the way in which the dancer steps on to the ball of the foot or on to pointe, with the body balanced in the correct position.

première first.

quart quarter.

quatrième fourth.

relever to rise up on the feet.

révérence a bow or curtsey.

rond de jambe a rounded movement of the leg.

sauter to jump.

seconde second.

sur le côté to the side.

sur place in one place.

temps time.

tendu stretched.

terre à terre close to the ground.

tour a turn.

tourner to turn.

turn-out the turning out of the legs from the hips; in ballet this is *gradually* worked up to turn-out of 180 degrees.

tutu the bodiced, frilled skirt worn by a ballet dancer; it can be of various lengths, ending on the thighs or near the ankle.

Index

Enjoying Ballet *by Jean Richardson*

Whether you know a lot, a little or nothing at all about ballet, this book will help you to understand it better and enjoy it more. The author traces the historical background of ballet and explains how dance, drama, music, costumes and scenery combine to make a whole. She describes some of today's great dance companies and most popular ballets and gives biographies of the dancers you may see performing. You can also find out what it's like to be a pupil in one of the top ballet schools and read how famous dancers of past and present started their careers.

Enjoying Music *by Jean Richardson*

Whether you're tone-deaf or able to tell if it's Karajan or Davis conducting with your eyes closed, this book will enable you to get more out of music. It will increase your knowledge of the history and technicalities of music as well as the whole range of orchestral instruments, composers – from Henry Purcell to Andrew Lloyd Webber – musical forms, and even tell you where to hear music live.

More Beaver Books

We hope you have enjoyed this Beaver Book. Here are some of the other titles:

Enjoying Ballet A Beaver original. Jean Richardson's survey of the history of ballet and today's best-known companies, performances and stars, illustrated with black and white photographs and with a foreword by Anthony Dowell of The Royal Ballet

Show-Biz Quiz A Beaver original. Test your knowledge of show business and its stars with this fun book by Robin May; illustrated by John Adams

Deadly Nightshade Sixteen stories of horror chosen by Peter Haining, in all of which children and darkness are important elements

Versicles and Limericks A Beaver original. An unsmiling aardvark and a confused centipede rub shoulders with Mona Lisa and Edward the Confessor in this collection of funny verses, limericks, riddles and clerihews by Charles Connell. Illustrated by Toni Goffe

These and many other Beavers are available at your local bookshop or newsagent, or can be ordered direct from: Hamlyn Paperback Cash Sales, PO Box 11, Falmouth, Cornwall TR10 9EN. Send a cheque or postal order, made payable to The Hamlyn Publishing Group, for the price of the book plus postage at the following rates: UK: 22p for the first book plus 10p a copy for each extra book ordered to a maximum of 92p;
BFPO and EIRE: 22p for the first book plus 10p a copy for the next 6 books and thereafter 4p a book;
OVERSEAS: 30p for the first book and 10p for each extra book.

New Beavers are published every month and if you would like the *Beaver Bulletin*, which gives a complete list of books and prices, including new titles, send a large stamped addressed envelope to:

Beaver Bulletin
The Hamlyn Group
Astronaut House
Feltham
Middlesex TW14 9AR

315177